WORDS ON THE PAGE, THE WORLD IN YOUR HANDS

BOOK ONE

Edited by
CATHERINE LIPKIN
and
VIRGINIA SOLOTAROFF

BOOK ONE

WORDS ON THE PAGE, THE WORLD IN YOUR HANDS

Prose and poetry written, selected, and adapted by contemporary writers for adults in literacy programs and others who wish to expand their reading horizons

PERENNIAL LIBRARY

HARPER & ROW, PUBLISHERS, NEW YORK
GRAND RAPIDS, PHILADELPHIA, ST. LOUIS, SAN FRANCISCO
LONDON, SINGAPORE, SYDNEY, TOKYO, TORONTO

To receive the complimentary teaching manual for *Words on the Page, The World in Your Hands*, please write to Department 361, Harper & Row, Publishers, 10 East 53rd Street, New York, NY 10022.

Grateful acknowledgment is made to Thomas M. Disch for the suggestion for the title *Words on the Page, The World in Your Hands*.

Copyright acknowledgments begin on p. 112.

WORDS ON THE PAGE, THE WORLD IN YOUR HANDS: BOOK ONE. Copyright © 1990 by Catherine Lipkin and Virginia Solotaroff. All rights reserved. Printed in the United States of America. No part of this book may be used or reproduced in any manner whatsoever without written permission except in the case of brief quotations embodied in critical articles and reviews. For information address Harper & Row, Publishers, Inc., 10 East 53rd Street, New York, NY 10022.

FIRST EDITION

Designed by Barbara DuPree Knowles

LIBRARY OF CONGRESS CATALOGING-IN-PUBLICATION DATA

Words on the page, the world in your hands / Catherine Lipkin & Virginia Solotaroff, eds.
   p. cm.
  ISBN 0-06-055154-2 (v. 1)   ISBN 0-06-096367-0 (pbk.: v. 1)
  ISBN 0-06-055155-0 (v. 2)   ISBN 0-06-096368-9 (pbk.: v. 2)
  ISBN 0-06-055156-9 (v. 3)   ISBN 0-06-096369-7 (pbk.: v. 3)
  1. Readers for new literates. 2. American literature—20th century. I. Lipkin, Catherine. II. Solotaroff, Virginia.
PE1126.A4W6   1990
428.6'2—dc19   88-45952

90 91 92 93 94 CC/FG 10 9 8 7 6 5 4 3 2 1
90 91 92 93 94 CC/FG 10 9 8 7 6 5 4 3 2 1 (pbk.)

CONTENTS

INTRODUCTION   x

WHAT I WANT   1
   ⇜ *Shirley Kaufman*

TO RECITE EVERY DAY   2
   ⇜ *William Stafford*

ELEGY   3
   ⇜ *James D. Houston*

INVITATION   9
   ⇜ *Sally Ann Drucker*

THE ARCH   10
   ⇜ *Shirley Kaufman*

LOVERS IN MIDDLE AGE   11
   ⇜ *Donald Hall*

IN JANUARY, 1962   12
   ⇜ *Ted Kooser*

v

THE WIDOW LESTER 13
ಆ§ *Ted Kooser*

HE SAID: 14
ಆ§ *Alice Walker*

AND THAT WAS IT 15
ಆ§ *Sharon Thompson*

HOUSECLEANING 23
ಆ§ *Nikki Giovanni*

MARKET ADVISER 24
ಆ§ *A. R. Ammons*

APPLE CORE 25
ಆ§ *Clarence Major*

FIRST LIGHT 27
ಆ§ *Charles Baxter*

HAPPINESS 34
ಆ§ *Stephen Dunn*

GOODBYE, SHEP 35
ಆ§ *Vesle Fenstermaker*

LOYALTY 43
ಆ§ *William Stafford*

IN MEMORY OF OUR CAT, RALPH   44
     ⁌ *Garrison Keillor*

AFTER CONVERSATION   46
     ⁌ *Paula Fox*

STRANGER   49
     ⁌ *Donald Hall*

TO STELLA   50
     ⁌ *John Hollander*

THE NIGHT YOUR DRESS LIFTED   51
     ⁌ *Stuart Dybek*

ALONE   52
     ⁌ *Nikki Giovanni*

COVER ME OVER   53
     ⁌ *Richard Eberhardt*

WHERE ARTHUR IS   54
     ⁌ *Vesle Fenstermaker*

REFLECTIVE   63
     ⁌ *A. R. Ammons*

SMALL SONG   64
     ⁌ *A. R. Ammons*

FEAR   65
   ◆§ *Charles Simic*

IF YOU CALL ME   66
   ◆§ *Shirley Kaufman*

BY NIGHT   67
   ◆§ *Robert Francis*

BABY ON THE BEACH   68
   ◆§ *Alix Kates Shulman*

STILLS   73
   ◆§ *A. R. Ammons*

SEPARATION   74
   ◆§ *W. S. Merwin*

WHEN MY FATHER DIED   75
   ◆§ *Sharon Olds*

WHILE I SLEPT   77
   ◆§ *Robert Francis*

NEXT DOOR   78
   ◆§ *Vesle Fenstermaker*

CAROLINE   80
   ◆§ *Linda Pastan*

ADAM'S COMPLAINT   81
    Denise Levertov

BOARDING HOUSE   82
    Ted Kooser

A VERY SPECIAL CHRISTMAS   83
    Nikki Giovanni

PAINTING THE GATE   86
    May Swenson

AT THE PLAYGROUND   88
    William Stafford

FREEDOM MARCH   89
    Dick Gregory

POLITICIAN   94
    John Keeble

LIGHTS   102
    Stuart Dybek

BRANDY'S STORY   103
    Ted Solotaroff

AFTER A WINTER'S SILENCE   111
    May Sarton

INTRODUCTION

José Garcia, a construction worker in his early thirties, came into a basic literacy program almost visibly trailing his shame. "I'm dumb," he said, without looking up. "I can't write." Neither could he read—in English or in Spanish, his native tongue—though he knew the alphabet, could print well, and his daughter, an alert second-grader, had started coaching him to read. He was, in fact, intelligent and ambitious, willing to come to an evening class following a workday that began at six in the morning.

At their first meeting, his tutor recorded the names of his work tools and his account of the tasks he performed with each of them. He was able to read these brief paragraphs. In meetings that followed, he spoke about his family and his school experience and was able to read an "autobiography" written in the words he had used to tell his story. His speaking vocabulary was becoming his reading vocabulary. He could soon read a simple story and, if it was in some way meaningful to him, learn its new words.

He was unable, however, to read and remember lists of unrelated vocabulary words—they meant nothing to him. And he was unwilling to read primers—"Run, Ken, run fast. You saw Igor take the money. Now he will kill you." José was studying on tired time and had a pressing need to learn about the real world. He had no patience for material he felt was trivial or meaningless.

The day he came in, tossed the "thriller" on the library table, and said, "I'm giving this back to you," was Martin Luther King's birthday. Copies of "I Have a Dream" had been set out on the table. José chose King's speech to replace the story of a boy who captured a thief as the text for the evening's lesson.

His tutor read "I Have a Dream" aloud. She and José discussed its themes, and together they found and underlined its many rhythmic repetitions. As they went through the piece again, José was responsible for reading the refrains. They read it a third time, in unison. Then José (with minor promptings) read the speech by himself, although it was well above his designated "grade" level. He was reading and understanding real writing! The splasher was suddenly swimming, and he knew it. For the first time he looked directly at his tutor and thanked her for the lesson. And he took King's speech home to read to his wife and daughter.

That experience set our minds in motion by highlighting a serious problem we shared with other literacy teachers. We had very little reading material to offer our students that in any way matched the seriousness of their commitment to learn—not only to identify the words on a page, that essential beginning, but to relate those words to the concerns of their lives.

Jonathan Kozel wrote *Illiterate America* in 1985. By juxtaposing the two words of his title for, perhaps, the first time, he alerted the informed public to a looming national crisis. He told us that twenty-five million American adults could not read product identification labels, menus, or street signs and that an additional thirty-five million read "only at a level which is less than equal to the full survival needs of our society." "Together," he wrote, "these 60 million people represent more than one third of the entire adult population."

Certainly, underdeveloped reading skills are a severe vocational handicap. Just as surely, they impoverish the lives of those individuals who are thereby denied access to the information on which considered personal choices can be made. In recent years, as the social and human costs of illiteracy have come to light, government, industry, and trade unions have undertaken massive literacy programs. Their efforts have been constrained, however, by a scarcity of appropriate texts.

With few exceptions, the materials available for these programs have been written for children or have been developed by educators who, assuming that adults learn much as children do, emphasize phonics and word recognition, often at the expense of meaningful content. There is little juice or joy in a story written to incorporate a vocabulary list calibrated to early grade-level expectations. If literacy students are to experience the stimulation of thought and feeling and the strengthening of a sense of place in the human community that mature writing can engender, the texts they read must engage their adult imaginations and offer them opportunities to experience their surroundings in new ways.

How were we to provide such generative texts? We combed the literature, as others had done, and found only a handful of accessible poems and short prose passages and almost no extended work that was free of sophisticated reference, complex syntax, rare usage, or vocabulary that was well beyond the reach of inexperienced readers.

Having failed to find the texts we needed, we decided to write them ourselves. Guided by our good intentions, like others before us, we did so. We are okay writers, not good writers. We wrote okay stories, not good stories. Not good enough. Effort, pedagogical sensibility, and the best will in the world were no substitute for literary gift.

We decided to contact serious writers, several hundred of them, and ask for help. Their support for the project overwhelmed us. They responded to our suggestions, offered some of their own, and spread the word at writers' conferences. Those whose work did not lend itself to our needs suggested the names of colleagues we might contact. We are grateful to all of them. Through their generous efforts we have been able to gather the texts we wanted—good stories and poems that, in their fidelity to the ambiguity and truth of lived lives, reach out with their strange yet somehow familiar burdens. In weighted moments of recognition (for who has not lived through some version of the conflict, betrayal, innocence, joy, and despair these works contain?), they offer something we know in part, and lead us to reexamine related aspects of our own lives. Literature invites a response. In formulating that response, perceptions are sharpened, sympathies are widened, thoughts are clarified. Learning takes place.

Rather than "writing down" to their readers, the distinguished authors in the Harper & Row collections have written *to* them. Some have selected pieces from their published works, some have created original work, and others, by judicious adaptation, have made their work more widely accessible without sacrificing flavor, point, or power. One can say, then, that *Words on the Page, The World in Your Hands* represents the literary community reaching out to the literacy community by offering memorable stories, poems, and essays that challenge, enlighten, and delight.

The Editors

WHAT I WANT
Shirley Kaufman

It's not what I say
  but what I don't say.

It's not what I get
  but what I don't get.

It's not what I do
  but what I don't do.

It's not what I wake up to
  but what I dream.

TO RECITE EVERY DAY
◆§ William Stafford

This bread is rye.
Many places the poor eat it,
for its grain grows anywhere
and makes a good gray flour.
You can eat it, from time to time.

Here are heavy shoes.
They last for years—
clumsy, yes, but strong and cheap.
They tramp to work early mornings.
Put them on.

Now stand up.
The old law says *work for pay*.
Try this shovel or this broom,
   just to see
      how it is
         for a while.

ELEGY

*Adapted by James D. Houston
from his book* The Men in My Life

At the county dump I am throwing away my father. His old paint rags, and stumps of brushes. Color charts. The spattered leather suitcase he used for so many years to carry the small tools and tiny jars of his trade, a suitcase so cracked and bent and buckle-ripped it's no good for anything now. I start to toss it on top of the brushes and rags, but hold back.

I toss instead the five-gallon drums that once held primer. He stacked them against one wall of his shop, for no good reason, kept dozens more than he would ever use. Around these I toss the bottles and tubes from his medicine chest. And cracked boots, filled with dust, as if in his closet it has been raining dust for years. And magazines. His fishing hat. Notes to himself:

Fix Window
Grease car
Call Harlow about job.

Bent nails in a jar, rolls of old wire, pipe sections, a fiddle he always intended to mend, old paid bills, check stubs, pencils his teeth chewed. Ragtag bits of this and that he had touched, stacked, stored. Useless to anyone but him, and he's gone now.

So I toss it all out there among the refrigerators and lettuce leaves, truck tires, busted sofas, and flowerpots. Onto that heap I throw my father, saving for the last that suitcase of his I'd first seen twenty years back—and it was old then—that day he took me out on a job for the first time, wearing a pair of his spattered overalls, rolled thick at the cuff, and a Sherwin-Williams white billcap.

"What're ya gonna do, Dad?" I say that first morning.

He doesn't answer. He never answers, as if he prefers silence. And I always wait, as if each silence is an exception, and this time he will turn and speak. It's my big reason for coming along this morning, the chance that out here on the job something might pass between us. I would never have been able to describe it ahead of time, but . . . maybe . . . something.

I wait and watch. Two minutes of puckering lips and long, slow blinks while he studies the labels, then he selects one tube, unscrews its top, and squeezes out a little on his fingertips.

I follow him to the five-gallon drum he's mixing paint in. A short stick of plywood holds the color he's shooting for—pale, pale green. He's proud of his eye for color, his knack for figuring just how pale this green will be when it dries. I watch and learn. Squeeze a green strip from the tube and stir it in, wide easy stirs while the green spirals out. Stir and stir. Then test: dip another stick in. Check the color. Stir.

"Okay, Jim. Take half this green paint and get that wall there covered."

He hands me a clean brush. Its black bristles shine with yesterday's thinner. He pours a gallon bucket full of paint for me and cuts the fall off clean.

"I'll be back in a minute," he says.

It's the first time I've painted anything away from home. I do not yet know that before summer is out I will dread the look of any long unpainted wall and wince at the smell of paint and thinner. But now I want this one to be a good job. I want to live up to the paint my dad has just mixed. I start by the living room door, taking my time, keeping the molding clear for a white trim later.

Ten minutes pass, and this first wall becomes my world. I am moving across the wide-open country—working my brush like Dad told me to, using the wrist, lapping strokes over—when I feel the need to turn around.

In the far doorway, the lady of the house stands glaring at me with a look of shock and anger. Next to the wall of her priceless living room she finds a kid dressed up in his father's overalls with the cuffs rolled thick. I realize how dangerous I look to her. Under my new green freckles my face turns scarlet.

The woman is gone.

From the hallway I hear her loud whisper. "Mr. Houston! That boy painting my living room couldn't be over fifteen!"

"He's thirteen, Ma'am."

"He's what?"

"It's my boy, Jim. He's giving me a hand this summer."

"I just wonder if he knows what he's doing in there."

"I painted my first house when I was ten."

"Well . . . I . . . if . . . I'd certainly be keeping an eye on him if I were you."

"Don't worry, Ma'am, he knows what to do."

Behind me I hear her walking slowly across the room. I keep painting; I don't look at her this time. Put plenty of paint on the brush. But don't let it run. Feather it at the overlap. Cover. Cover.

Dad comes in and fills up another gallon bucket and helps me finish the wall. He catches my eye once and winks. Then we are painting toward each other in a silence broken only by the whish of bristles and the cluck of brush handle against the can. Somewhere in the back of the house a radio is playing its faraway music.

We finish the room by quitting time. Dad looks over my work, finds a couple of bald spots along the baseboard, and has me fill these in, saying only, "Keep an eye out for them holidays." We clean the brushes. He drops the lid shut on his kit of a suitcase, snaps the buckle to, straps it, and says, "Might as well take that on out to the truck."

I had never paid much attention to his kit. Now I know just enough about what's inside for it to be mysterious. A year from now I will know too much about what's inside. By then I will be able to read his half smile, his apology for having only this to offer me. But today carrying it is an honor. No one has ever carried that kit but him. It has a manly weight, a fine weight for carrying from the house to the curb, for hoisting onto the truck bed. It lands with a *thunk* and sits solid.

I wait for Dad to tie his ladder on the overhead rack, and we climb into the cab. He winks once more as we prepare to leave Mrs. So-and-so behind. Reeking of paint and turpentine, we are Sherwin and Williams calling it a day, with no way to talk much over the rattle of his metal-floored Chevy, and no need to talk. The clutch leaps. Wind rushes in, mixing paint and gasoline fumes, and all you need to do is to stay loose for the jolts and the whole long rumble ride home.

At the county dump, I am throwing away my father, lifting his old suitcase to toss the last of him onto the smoking heap. It is crusted with splats of seventy colors now, its lid corners split as if somebody sat on it. The ragged straps dangle. One shred of leather holds the chromium buckle that still catches the sun where the paint doesn't cover it. The shred of leather gives. The buckle breaks. The kit flies open.

As if compressed inside, waiting to escape, the smell of oil and pigment cuts through the smoke and rot that fills the air around me. My throwing arm stays. My other hand reaches out. I'm holding the suitcase, inhaling the smell that always clung to him, even after he had scrubbed. It rose from the creases in his hands, from the white liners rimming his fingernails, from the paint specks he sometimes missed with the thinner at the corners of his eyes. I breath it in deep.

I close the suitcase slowly, prepare to heave it once and for all. This time with both hands, out and up. Out among all those things you find only by losing them.

One last glance. By five tonight this, too, will be gone for good, when the bulldozer comes to shove it over the side with the rest of today's collection—treasures of yesterday, old necessities, parts of the heart.

INVITATION
ಆ§ Sally Ann Drucker

I stumble
you halt
we sidestep,
not dancing yet.
You move backwards
toward me
I move sideways
toward you.
Tongue-tied,
trusting eyes,
we speak
in silence.

THE ARCH
✒ *Shirley Kaufman*

    Half the world leans
    on the other half
       to make it stand.

    That's how an arch
    stays up,
       two feet on land.

    That's why I feel
    so straight
       when you hold my hand.

LOVERS IN MIDDLE AGE
Donald Hall

The young girls look up
as we walk past the line at the movie,
and go back to looking at their fingernails.

Their boyfriends are combing their hair,
and chew gum
as if they meant to insult us.

Today we made love all day.
I look at you. You are smiling at the sidewalk,
dear wrinkled face.

IN JANUARY, 1962
Ted Kooser

With his hat on the table before him,
my grandfather waited until it was time
to go to my grandmother's funeral.
Beyond the window, his eighty-eighth winter
lay white in its furrows. The little creek
which cut through his cornfield was frozen.
Past the creek and the broken, brown stubble,
on a hill which thirty years before
he'd given the town, a green tent flapped
under the cedars. Throughout the day before,
he'd stayed there by the window, watching
the blue woodsmoke from the thawing-barrels
catch in the bitter wind and vanish,
and had seen, so small in the distance,
a man breaking the earth with a pick.
I suppose he could feel that faraway work
in his hands—the steel-smooth, cold oak handle;
the thick, dull shock at the wrists—
for the following morning, as we waited there,
it was as if it hurt him to move them,
those hard old hands which lay curled and still
near the soft gray felt hat on the table.

THE WIDOW LESTER
Ted Kooser

I was too old to be married,
but nobody told me.
I guess they didn't care enough.
How it had hurt, though, catching bouquets
all those years!
Then I met Ivan, and kept him,
and never knew love.
How his feet stunk in the bed sheets!
I could have told him to wash,
but I wanted to hold that stink against him.
The day he dropped dead in the field,
I was watching.
I was hanging up sheets in the yard,
and I finished.

HE SAID:
Alice Walker

He said: I want you to be happy.
He said: I love you so.
Then he was gone.
For two days I was happy.
For two days, he loved me so.
After that, I was on my own.

AND THAT WAS IT

Adapted from true experiences told to and recorded by Sharon Thompson

SADIE HAWKINS DANCE

My friend told me, "Ask him,"
and I go, "No,
how embarrassing for a girl to ask a guy
for a date."
And she asked him.

He goes, "Well,
doesn't she have
a mouth
for herself?"

And I felt like,
"Eeee, how embarrassing.
You shouldn't have
done that, you know."
And I go, "Well,
will you go?"
He goes, "Yeah."
So me and him went to the dance.

Okay, you go into the dance,
and they have this preacher or
pretend preacher, you know,
and they sit there with the book.

They have this pretend marriage license
worked out, you know, and you both sign it,
and you both, like, read the vows and that?
And they give you these paper rings.

And then they take you in this booth,
and you stay there for a minute.
Then he tells me,
"Let's get married."
I tell him,
"Oh, how embarrassing."

And everybody keeps telling us
get married,
like, you know,
do the thing.

So we did.
And I have that marriage license
all the time.
I put it in my room
and that was something to me.

AND THAT WAS IT

Maybe
I wanted
to find out.
Maybe I just
wanted to
get it
over with.
I don't know.

It was like—
psssst,
one minute here,
the next minute
there.
It happened.
And that was it.

With him
it seems like
he was already
an expert.
He's two years
younger than me,
but he's done it
many times;
at his school,
so I didn't know.

I keep thinking
to this day: why
did I do it?
I'm telling you
I did it
unconsciously, because
I wouldn't do
a thing
like that.

HOW MY MOTHER FOUND OUT

I was going to
take a bath.
And like
my breasts was big.
So she found out that way.

Well, me being scared
and all,
I kept saying, "No,"
until I just
stopped
and said, "Yeah," and
started crying like
there was no
tomorrow.

HIS PARENTS

    See,
    in Puerto Rico
    the guys are taller,
    you know.
    He was tall,
    yet he was
    young.

    His parents felt—
    they were saying that
    the girls
    over here
    are tramps,
    stuff like that.
    The girls do it,
    they say,
    then blame
    one of the guys
    from over there.

His parents like own a company
and they own a pretty big house.
They pay maids to come and clean it,
stuff like that.
So I think they're pretty wealthy.
They could support the kid, you know.

The World in Your Hands

I mean, it's their grandson.
But nooooo.

So they don't want to?
I don't want them, either.

I said,
"Forget it.
We don't need their money.
All I care
is about the kid.
He comes with us,
He's *ours,* not theirs."

THE WAY IT IS NOW

That's the way it is now.
They ask,
"How's the baby?"
Now that's stupid.
First they don't want
to give us
his name.
Then they don't want
to support
his baby.

And now they're asking,
"How's the baby?"

"Who does he look like?"
and stuff. I mean, *come on!*

I couldn't say
what we did
was a long-time thing.
I mean,
we only did it
a few minutes.
Let's put it this way:
It just takes
a few minutes
to be broken.

I was,
like I said,
doing it unconsciously,
and I couldn't even say
how it feels.

And I couldn't say that
he was a nice guy.
I mean,
he wasn't,
you know.

After that, nothing;
no more looking at each other
and stuff like that.

Him and me,
it wasn't
a big thing.

So—I hope
through the years to come,
who knows?
Find me a good husband,
a father to my son,
something like that.

But not
yet.

HOUSECLEANING
Nikki Giovanni

i always liked housecleaning
even as a child
i dug straightening
the cabinets
putting new paper on
the shelves
washing the refrigerator
inside out
and unfortunately this habit has
carried over and i find
i must remove you
from my life

MARKET ADVISER
A. R. Ammons

If you're
not in

it for
the ups

and downs
you might

as well
get out

of it
she said

APPLE CORE
Clarence Major

Up the road
I saw black birds
on the edge of a pine box.
When I got there
the birds flew a few feet away,
to the other side.
I looked down in the box.
There were red apples,
ripe, with stems still on them.
A sign on the box said Take One.
So I took one.
My, it was heavy,
and when I bit into it,
you would not believe
such sweetness. I walked on,
eating it down to the core.
When I finished, I threw the core
out over a cornfield.
A bird flew to catch it
before it hit the ground,
but it fell anyway.
The bird followed.

And I stood there,
not seeing anything
but the stalks moving
in the morning wind.
I waited, and the bird
came up, carrying the core.
He flew off across the field,
carrying this thing,
about twice the size
   of his own head.

FIRST LIGHT
*Adapted by Charles Baxter
from his novel* First Light

"Hugh. Wake up." Hugh is in bed. His father bends over him to shake him. This is the morning for the first trip to the hospital. Hugh tugs at his pillow and at the stuffed dragon he sleeps with. His father tells him to shake a leg. His father's breath smells of the night. It smells of cigarettes and toothpaste. Hugh pulls the bedspread aside and places his feet on the cold wood floor. With his father's help he lowers his pajamas down and raises his T-shirt up. Even in the warmth of morning, Hugh feels cold and hugs himself. Hugh's father puts his son's clean clothes out. Then he yanks at the window shade. Beyond the front lawn of the house is the sun, streaming through Hugh's window across the floor. Rubbing his eyes, the boy walks into the bathroom to pee. He remembers to flush and then to wash his hands. He is careful. His mother is gone, and he wants to please his father.

Downstairs, his father has made him scrambled eggs and bacon and toast. The eggs have garlic powder all over them. Hugh smears jam on his toast. He has remembered to put the napkin in his lap, but he still spills a gob of jam on his shirt. His father sees it and says, "That's all right. But we'll have to find you a clean shirt. We can't have you going into the hospital looking like that."

"Daddy?" Hugh asks.

"What?"

"How soon will we go?"

"Right after breakfast," his father says.

After Hugh puts on a clean shirt, the boy and his father leave for the hospital. Hugh sits in front. The dashboard is so high that he has to stretch to see anything. He can't remember being up this early. No one is in the yards or in the stores. When they drive by the lake, no one is out there fishing or swimming. Hugh sits back and watches the telephone wires.

"Are you excited?" his father asks.

"I guess so."

"She's beautiful. You're going to love her."

"I know."

"You'll see. Don't worry. You've never been in a hospital before, have you?"

"No."

"It's not so scary. Really. You'll get used to it right away."

"Is Mommy okay?"

"She's fine. She can't wait to see you. She asked me last night to tell you how much she was looking forward to seeing you this morning."

Hugh sits and wonders what he will tell his sister

once she is old enough to talk. He can't think of what he will say. She might not like him. She might go through life ignoring him and thinking he's a creep.

At last they park at the county hospital, three floors high, with a long sidewalk leading to the parking lot. Hugh sees that his father's hand is shaking. Out in the light of the parking lot, Hugh hears his father say, "Well, shall we go in, Chief?" Hugh has an odd feeling that he is spinning. But it's not enough to make you sick, not like what the kids do at birthday parties where they blindfold you and whip you around to pin the tail on the donkey. This is more like someone turning your body so slowly you don't quite notice you're being turned. Hugh knows what it is. He is feeling the earth itself turning, moving from night to day. He feels it under his feet.

"Are you coming, kiddo?" his father asks, looking back at him. "Are you coming in to see her, or are you just going to stand there?" His father takes his hand. He closes his fingers around his father's hand and watches as his father pulls a cigarette out with his other hand from his jacket pocket. He lights it, takes a puff, then snuffs it out on the sidewalk.

Inside the hospital, Hugh breathes in. One breath tells him that this is a terrible place. The hospital smells of terror and pain. He's never smelled anything like it; maybe basements and plumbing, but it's worse than that. It makes his hair stand up. He walks with his father down the yellow hallways. They go past the front desk and the smiling woman who sees his father but not him.

His father opens a door to the stairs. Hugh goes inside. The stairs are gray. There is a bare light bulb on the ceiling, and it makes his father's shadow stretch out as they climb the stairs to the second floor.

On the second floor, Hugh's father holds the door open. One of the nurses sees Hugh, and she shakes her head. "No children," she says. "No children on this floor." Then she looks over at Hugh's father. She knows him, and she says his name. She and his father talk for a moment. Then she goes to a closet and returns with a surgical mask. She covers Hugh's nose and mouth with it. "This is so you don't spread germs," she says. "This one time."

"What's that smell?" Hugh asks. He is walking by flowers in a vase at the nurses' station. "Daddy, what's that smell?"

"Pretty bad, isn't it?" his father says. "It's ether. They don't use ether much here. They use it in the operating rooms. But not for mothers. They use it on other people."

They are passing by doors now. Some of the doors are open, but Hugh doesn't look inside. He is afraid he will see people lying on their backs, holding out their hands. He wants to run out, but his father still holds on to him, and where would he run to? The sun is shining through all the windows on the hallway's east side. Hugh has to walk through the sunlight to get to where his mother lies. She will be lying back in bed, he knows. Her eyes will be closed, and this baby will be beside her that she and his father have somehow brought from somewhere into this world.

His father stops near a corner area. There are hard green chairs near a window. His father squats down and faces Hugh. Hugh is afraid that his father is going to tell him off. But no. In a voice that is so low that Hugh can hardly hear it, his father tells Hugh that he loves him. He says that he will always love him and that he is a wonderful boy. He tells him that he has a sister now, and he'll have to love her and take care of her. Hugh says, "Daddy, what did I do?"

"You didn't do anything," his father says. "Let's go in."

Hugh's father knocks twice on the door to the room, Number 252. Hugh hears his mother's voice say, "Come in." Hugh pushes at the door, and from right to left his mother's room becomes visible at last.

"My two men," his mother says. She looks at Hugh. "My two *masked* men." Beyond his mother's bed is another window. It faces east into the sun. Sunlight is streaming from behind his mother into the room. All the room's objects are bright—the glass of water, the box of tissues, the vase of flowers on the windowsill. They are red and white flowers whose names Hugh doesn't know. They might be roses, roses for love.

"Hugh," his mother says. "Don't stand there back by the door. Come in. Come see."

She smiles again. Hugh doesn't know what he has done to deserve the smile. Now he walks forward into the room. The sunlight from the window hurts his eyes. His mother is wearing white hospital clothes, and something has happened to her eyes, even though she's smiling now. Her hair is combed in a new way. It is pulled back and hardly parted at all. Her skin is pale. "Mom," Hugh says, rushing forward to kiss her.

But now he sees *her*, inside his mother's right arm. Hugh stops. He sees the blond hair on his sister's head. As his mother holds his sister up into the sunlight, she says, "This is Dorsey."

"Dorsey," Hugh repeats.

"We named her last night," Hugh's father says.

"Come closer, Hugh. Come closer."

Hugh's feet take him nearer the bed. He looks up toward his mother. "Can I see her hands?" he asks.

"Of course," his mother says. Slowly, she unwraps the blanket from around the baby's arms, first the right arm and then the left. His sister's skin in the morning sunlight is almost yellow, with small streaks of purple. Hugh feels himself moving toward her. As he says her name, "Dorsey," he holds his right hand out, his finger pointing down. His sister's skin is the quietest thing he's ever seen. It hardly seems part of the world at all. She yawns, opening and closing her tiny hands, the size of toy glass marbles. "Come closer," his mother says again.

Her voice seems to come not from her mouth but from the room itself, the earth, and the air. With his right hand in front of him, his finger still pointing out and down, Hugh reaches forward and with unpracticed tenderness touches his sister's hand for the first time.

HAPPINESS
Stephen Dunn

A state you must dare not enter
 with hopes of staying,
quicksand in the marshes, and all

the roads leading to a castle
 that doesn't exist.
But there it is, as promised,

with its perfect bridge above
 the crocodiles,
and its doors forever open.

GOODBYE, SHEP
Vesle Fenstermaker

When I came home from my job at the Well-Baby Clinic, Mama was playing her opera records again and looking through the old green photograph album. At least she wasn't crying.

I picked up the spray can and fizzed it all around the piano. Its fake flower odor doesn't really erase the old-dog stink.

Shep, panting under the piano, looked up at me. The hairs of his tail moved slightly. Yellow cords of matter filled the tired curves of his cloudy eyes.

I patted his head. "Hi, Shep," I said, entering the field of his strong breath, trapped beneath the piano.

Mama watched me, frowning. "He was a good boy today," she said. She closed the album and smoothed her hair and her dress with pale fingers. "You used to love him so," she said. "Remember the time you called from Brownie camp just to talk to Shep?"

I remembered. For a minute I wanted the golden haze that touches us both when Mama lays open the past she remembers. She smiles then, and says, always, "Old happy times." And I feel it too. Papa alive and the boys home and me a child and no trouble.

I handed her the evening paper. "Finish listening to the opera, darling," I said. "I'll fix supper."

I called Shep to follow me, but he only stretched his long head out along the dark floor.

I closed the kitchen door and let Buff in. Buff is a younger collie, a nice dog and good to Shep.

At supper Mama looked fragile, tired. "Eat, Mama," I said.

Mama knows I want her to stop teaching, take it easy, get rid of the dogs, get an apartment. But some nights, like this, I just can't fuss with her. We made plans for the garden.

After supper I took Shep and Buff for a walk. Shep draws somehow on Buff's sharp energy. He watches Buff, lurches ahead in a sort of trot now and again, trying, trying, for just a few seconds. Buff leaps away, runs back, circles us both, and bounds off again.

Circling us like that, Buff gives us all the news, but Shep and I, we don't receive it. I, because I'm only human, and Shep, because he doesn't care anymore. Almost nothing reaches him now.

When we came in, Mama gave Shep his pills, cleaned his eyes, brushed him as much as he would let her, crooning to him all the while. Seeing her there, shoulders bent, quieting a restless Shep who seemed almost ready to snap at her, I knew suddenly what I had to do.

Slowly Mama straightened up. "There now, old sport. Off to bed. Dream of rabbits. Old happy times."

Glancing at me, she smiled faintly and went to her desk to grade papers.

I watched her lower her thin body onto the desk chair. Mama's one of the walking wounded. In all the grinding time since my father's death, I've seen her pay and pay for what they had. Is any happiness worth that, I ask myself, and shy away from men.

Everything here in this house—the album, the books they shared, the furniture he used—reminds her to keep mourning. She needs to stay here in the midst of the reminders of his life, she says. She wants everything as it was when she was whole.

Especially Shep.

One day long ago, Shep was all mine, tied under the Christmas tree, bumping his short nose against the ornaments, a red ribbon nearly lost in his soft neck fur.

I hear my father laugh, deep and strong, while I squeal and run to the puppy. I say to Mama, who is beaming peace and joy, "He's fuzzy! He's fuzzy!"

Nothing else that Christmas was anything to anyone. Just Shep. Suddenly everywhere in the house. A laugh a minute. We competed to love him. Sometime every day I screamed at someone, "He's mine! He's mine!" But they knew better.

And now he smells. And leaks. And moans. And snaps. And Mama goes on tending his carcass, turning away from his pain.

The next day I came home from work early. It was

the afternoon of Mama's teachers' meeting. "Come on, dogs!" I said, tramping loudly into the living room. "Let's go swimming!"

Barking like gunshots, Buff chased his tail. "Get Shep!" I said. "Buff, get Shep!"

Buff dashed to where Shep lay on the window seat and nudged him. I leaned over them and said, "Gravel pit, Shep. Let's go, baby."

He raised his head and looked at me. I felt my stomach crawl inside. Then slowly he turned away, laying his ears back, coughing. Shep loves the gravel pit, loves to swim. I mean, he used to.

When I snapped his lead on, he sighed, shifting his long body, and heaved himself up. Carefully, he dropped off the window seat and thumped slowly to the door. Buff skittered and slid, trying to run against the pull of the leash.

It was a warm late-September day. Already reds and yellows marked the trees overhanging the gravel pit. I parked off the road and let Buff out. Immediately he ran, barking brightly, to begin his survey of the light weedy woods beyond the dry field toward the water.

I leaned into the back of the car. "Come on out, Shep. It's nice here." Shep looked at me blankly, and struggled to the ground, an old man going along with a child's game.

Shep and I trudged through the stubble, while far ahead Buff barked us on to the carnival of sun and autumn.

I guess Shep and I have walked or run a thousand miles together, but this time I seemed to be alone. I looked down at him. His nose was close to the ground, and his wide old body rocked from side to side as he moved along.

Ever since that long-ago Christmas morning I've been sure I understood Shep perfectly, sure that I sensed everything he learned and felt and was. I knew him as part of myself, the joyful guiltless simple part. Now, walking the same path, we were not together at all.

Carefully, Shep and I made a track through the weeds down to the muddy bank. Already Buff was slopping through the shallow water, snapping at dragonflies, pawing water-skaters, tasting the leaf-scented air.

At the water's edge we stopped. Shep stood panting. Then, slowly, he lowered his head to the water and lifted one paw to touch its surface.

I stood and watched the dogs. Why had I come? For Shep, one last swim? For Shep, one last roll in the lovely, odorous woods?

But there wasn't any Shep, really. Only a mass of aching flesh dragged out of its piano cave into the harsh sunlight of an old game I was playing.

I lifted my arms in the wind and told myself this pain will end when my terrible task is done.

Now Buff was swimming in the sun-patterned water, rolling his eyes at the sky, his long nose a prow in the ripples.

I leaned over. "Shep," I said, "swim with Buff. Swim, Shep."

I put my hand on his dry, heavy coat, halfheartedly pushing him toward the water. He stood, heavy and motionless, with his head down.

My eyes misted and I moved my hand to scratch his neck. "No, baby, don't try it. Rest in the sun. Rest."

In a little while the air began to chill with evening. Buff leaped out of the water at last, slithering in the mud, sleek and dark and ready to shake. He went straight to Shep, nudged him, and stood over him, his head cocked. But Shep lay still, eyelids drooping, a long brown-and-white lump facing the water.

I shooed Buff away from us before he shook himself, and I let him roll in the leaves as much as he wanted to, not minding at all the long brushing I'd have to do later.

Suddenly I was very tired. "Come on, fellows, time to go," I said softly. Gently I pushed Shep up the last steep bit of the bank and stayed beside him while he walked, slowly, slowly, to the car.

I drove straight to the kennel, blinking my eyes and setting my jaw. As soon as I turned off the main road, Buff began to whine, nosing my shoulder. But on the back seat, Shep lay quite still.

After I parked the car I snapped Buff's lead on firmly. He whined and pawed at my hand. "No, Buff, none of that. You have to help me. Out, now, out!"

Holding Buff's lead with one hand, I tugged at Shep's collar. "Come along, Shep. It's time now." My voice was steady. In a few minutes it would be behind me.

Shep and I and Buff walked into the kennel.

Dr. Carter said, "Hello, Annie." He patted my shoulder. "It's Shep, isn't it?" I nodded. "I thought you'd come soon."

He leaned over Shep and stroked him with long, tender strokes. "Okay, boy. It's all right. Good dog. Good old dog."

Buff, very quiet now, had wound himself around a small chair.

Dr. Carter said, "Just go along home, Annie. It's better. Come back next week and look at the puppies. Would you like me to call your mother?"

Not looking at Dr. Carter, I unwound Buff from the chair. "No, thanks," I said.

Murmuring to Shep and stroking him, Dr. Carter led him through the door of the lab. As his body moved out of sight, I whispered, "Goodbye, Shep."

I jerked at Buff's leash and left the kennel.

Mama pushed Buff away when we came into the house. "Where did you go? Where's Shep?"

As she looked at me, her face changed, and I saw that she knew. I kissed her and held her. "Chasing rabbits, Mama," I said. "Chasing rabbits."

Slowly she moved out of my arms and sat down in

a deep chair. I put Buff in the yard. When I came back, Mama hadn't moved. She looked as if she'd been pushed into the chair.

"How could you?" she said. "How could you bring yourself to do it?"

I shrugged and sat on the floor beside her, leaning my head against her knee.

She smoothed my hair. In the quiet of the room, I heard Buff barking outside. At last Mama said, "You were right. You were strong." She sighed. "I knew. Oh, I knew, but I couldn't do it. There was never any day when I could."

She choked a little and swallowed. "It's funny how things change, isn't it? For a long, long time I took care of you." She closed her eyes. "And now you'll take care of me. You'll do the things for me that I can't do for myself."

I turned my face into the soft folds of her skirt, and I cried for Shep and Mama and me.

LOYALTY
William Stafford

Some people,
they tire of their dog,
   they get a divorce.
Their car breaks down,
   they trade it in.
A sweater gets a hole
in the elbow,
   they throw it away—
        I take thee, Rover,
        for better, for worse,
        in sickness and in health,
        for richer, for poorer,
        till death do us part.

IN MEMORY OF OUR CAT, RALPH
Garrison Keillor

When we got home, it was almost dark.
Our neighbor waited on the walk.
"I'm sorry, I have bad news," he said.
"Your cat, the gray-black one, is dead.
I found him by the garbage an hour ago."
"Thank you," I said, "for letting us know."

We dug a hole in the flower bed
With lilac bushes overhead,
Where this cat loved to lie in spring
And roll in dirt and eat the green
Delicious first spring buds,
And laid him down and covered him up,
Wrapped in a piece of tablecloth,
Our good old cat laid in the earth.

We quickly turned and went inside
The empty house and sat and cried
Softly in the dark some tears
For that familiar voice, that fur,
That soft weight missing from our laps,
That we had loved too well perhaps

And mourned from weakness of the heart:
A childish weakness, to regard
An animal whose life is brief
With such affection and such grief.

If such is weakness, so it be.
This modest elegy
Is only meant to note the death
Of one cat so we won't forget
His face, his name, his gift
Of cat affection while he lived,
The sweet shy nature
Of this graceful creature,
The simple pleasure of himself,
The memory of our cat, Ralph.

AFTER CONVERSATION
⇜§ *Adapted by Paula Fox from her book* One-Eyed Cat

Ned went in to see his mother almost every day, even if it was only for a minute or two. At first he would have a conversation with her that was not so different from the ones he had with other grownups—his teacher, Miss Jefferson, or members of his father's congregation. If he could spend a good long time with her, the conversation would change. He would get a little stool and take it next to the wheelchair and sit down on it. He would tell her what he had done that day, what he had seen, and even what he had thought. That was what she seemed most interested in.

When he brought her wildflowers in the spring and summer, she told him the names of each one. If he found an odd stone, she could name what minerals were in it. If he described a bird, she could sometimes tell him its name. When that was done, and the flowers had been put aside with the stone, she would ask him what he thought about.

"What's outside of everything?" he asked her once.

"Outside the earth?"

"I mean the sky. What's outside of the sky and the stars?"

"No one knows," she said.

"There must be something," he said. "There can't be nothing, can there?"

"Your father would say God," she said.

"What would you say?" he asked, a little troubled, and interested that she had a different idea from his father.

"The thought of it is too strange to fit inside my brain," she said. "Maybe it is like the set of wooden dolls your uncle brought you back from Hungary when you were little. Do you remember? There must have been ten of them, each fitting inside another until the smallest one, which was no bigger than your fingernail. In the universe, perhaps the dolls go on forever, getting larger and larger."

Ned always knew when his mother was getting tired. He would see a slight tightening of a muscle in her cheek that was as soft as the flannel of his oldest pajamas. There was something clothlike about her skin. It made him sad for a moment, though he didn't know why.

He didn't often think of his mother as an invalid. But when he went to visit a school friend or to spend an afternoon with a boy from Sunday school, he was surprised at the great noise and thundering in the house, at his friend's shouting, "Mom!" and banging doors and slamming windows and thumping up and down stairs. It was so different at home. Ned couldn't remember when he had learned to walk softly. He was pretty sure no one could make less noise than he did. If he brought someone home to play with—that did not happen often—they stayed outside or, if it was raining, on the porch.

"When did you get sick?" Ned asked his mother once when the conversation part was finished and they were really talking. He had just touched the skirt of her dress; she always wore bright, pretty dresses.

"When you were about five years old," she had answered. "But I think the sickness had been coming on for a long while."

"Before that could you run fast?"

"Yes, I could run and run. And I rode my horse, Cosmo. I could pick you up and swing you in the air."

"Then—" he began.

His mother opened her eyes and turned to look at him.

"Then the ax fell," she said.

The ax fell. He repeated the words to himself now. She had been like a tree, he thought, and then was cut down.

STRANGER
Donald Hall

A boy who played and talked and read with me
Fell from a maple tree.

I loved her, but I told her I did not,
And wept, and then forgot.

I walked the streets where I was born and grew,
And all the streets were new.

TO STELLA
John Hollander

Stella (your name means "star")
   at the starry sky
     You stare with those
two shining eyes of blue.

I wish I were black midnight
   there up high,
     With millions of eyes
all looking down at you.

THE NIGHT YOUR DRESS LIFTED
Stuart Dybek

There was a burst
of static
on radios
all over the city

the night your dress
lifted over your head

and in the dark
its wool combed
fireworks from your hair.

ALONE
Nikki Giovanni

i can be
alone by myself
i was alone
lonely alone
now i'm lonely
with you
something is wrong
there are flies
everywhere
i go

COVER ME OVER
Richard Eberhardt

Cover me over, clover;
Cover me over, grass.
The mellow day is over
And there is night to pass.

Green arms about my head,
Green fingers on my hands.
Earth has no quieter bed
In all her quiet lands.

WHERE ARTHUR IS
Vesle Fenstermaker

My mother does the best she can for her two boys, me and my brother, Dean. She manages by lying to my father and stealing from him. It's interesting that things that are supposed to be bad can work out okay.

Whenever she lies to my father she looks straight at him and opens her eyes wide. She looks like a doll that isn't really seeing. She tells the lie she needs to tell quickly. If he was listening, my father would hear that her voice is different, but he never is.

She has a system for stealing too. I heard her take the money for this typewriter out of his pants bit by bit, late at night. I heard her because I always lie awake waiting for the bedspring noise to be over. As soon as my father begins to snore, I hear her get out of bed, real slow and easy. I can almost hear her lift his pants off the chair, and then there's the soft rustling of bills and the small sound of coins before she quiets them. Sometimes the belt buckle clinks when she puts the pants back on the chair and the bed creaks again as she eases back down.

When she told him that Uncle Harry gave me the typewriter she cocked her head like a little bird and made her mouth young, but her eyes stayed the same.

Now I have two safe places. In the afternoon I go to the library—where Arthur is—and at night I have my typewriter here in the basement.

Today my brother Dean left. I knew he would sometime. He doesn't understand anything and he's afraid of everything, especially Papa.

The thing is, Annabelle Santini, down the block, is pregnant. She says it's Dean's baby. He says he doesn't even like Annabelle.

When I got home from the library, my mother and Dean were sitting in the kitchen. He was crying. My mother sat and stared at her hands spread out on the oilcloth. Her mouth was a straight line, and she kept saying, "Your father will kill you. He'll kill you."

Dean looked awful. I left.

When we had supper, Papa was quiet for a while, drinking beer and eating fast the way he does. Then all three of them started yelling at each other. Nobody looked at me. Each one kept glancing at the other two and then back at the table as if it were home base or something.

Dean said that Annabelle didn't really know, it could have been a lot of guys, and that he hadn't even lived yet.

I wonder how Dean imagines his life beginning. When does it start? Who will he be then?

I stared at a hole in the oilcloth while they kept yelling mean stuff at each other. The thing they didn't mention, the thing Dean forgot, is that Annabelle's father is Papa's foreman.

"Listen, Papa, you don't know—" Dean said.

Papa laughed. "The hell I don't. I *been* there, stupid."

Then Papa pushed back his chair. He went to the dish drainer and picked up a carving knife. He squinted at Dean and smiled. "Listen, kid," he said. "Let me do you a big favor. I'll cut the damn thing off. How about that?"

Mama giggled like a crazy person. Then she said to Papa, "Don't upset yourself, Roy."

Dean screamed and ran out the door.

I left too. The look of the knife was making me sick.

At the library this afternoon I was going to tell Arthur about it, but I didn't. It hurts Arthur—I can see it—when things at my house get to me. I don't like the shadow on his face when I have trouble. It's funny, because nothing else at all bothers him.

Arthur works at the library and goes to college at night. He's very tall and calm. I figure he's really a Watusi, one of the tall Africans, like in the *National Geographic*. He looks out over people's heads, over all the clashing and hurting. Even the color of his skin is calm, like an old leather binding that will go on and on after other things wear themselves out.

Arthur has some interesting ideas about what I'm going to be. When I grow up. Arthur says, I'll probably be a rare-book dealer. He's noticed that I like to hold books in my hands, just heft them and feel them.

Today I had lunch at school with Laurie. I told her how I felt about Annabelle and Dean. Thinking out loud, really. I do that a lot with Laurie. I hear what I say to her, and then I know what I think.

Laurie is small, with black hair and nice eyes. Her face comes to me when I'm reading romantic stuff, and I imagine us together when we're older.

"How come Annabelle and Dean don't even like each other anymore?" I ask her.

"You know Dean. He's scared, as usual," she said. "And how can Annabelle like anybody? Her mother hits her, and she's sick every morning in the girls' room. She pretends she doesn't know what happened."

For the first time Laurie was no help at all. In fact, as Arthur says, *au contraire.* She seemed to be imagining herself in Annabelle's trouble. Mad at Dean and at me too. It was like she and Annabelle were on one side and me and Dean on the other. Which was silly. Laurie and I are alike, friends, and not like the other two at all.

Arthur and I went to the park today. Some people we passed stared at us. Was it because he's black and I'm white? Or were they the kind who are suspicious of two male people together? Who cares? Life is too thick to be worrying about people's eyes sliding over you.

We ate ice cream cones. He had vanilla and I had chocolate, which we laughed about. The whole black and

The World in Your Hands

white thing is nothing but boring to Arthur. He says that being black, he's already more than white, and that now he's working on the next step. He won't tell me what that is. "Think, David," he says. "Why should I tell you what you can figure out for yourself?" We threw the ends of our cones to some ducks and sat down on a bench.

Arthur said, "Listen, kid, I'm not going to be around anymore. I found a job near school."

That's all he would tell me. I tried to imagine the library without him. The college he goes to is way on the other side of town. He lives by himself, but I don't know where.

"We can meet sometimes, right?" I said. "Eat Chinese or something?"

Arthur looked over my head at the trees. "No, David," he said, still not looking at me. "It's no good to stay in one little slot and get pinned down in it. You have to move along, meet other people, see other places."

"That's why we can't eat Chinese?"

He didn't think that was funny. "Right," he said. He frowned and threw a twig in the water. "You just keep on reading and thinking and watching what's going on. Maybe we'll run into each other sometime. In Paris or Rome, maybe. Who knows?"

Arthur and I used to talk about going everywhere to track down all the writers we wanted to meet, to ask them questions.

I said, "I bet there really aren't so many people around to talk to."

Arthur looked at me then, but I wouldn't look at him. "Sure there are. You'll see. How's that girl, Laura?"

"Laurie," I said. Arthur never gets her name right. "Do you have a girl, Arthur?"

"No," he said, getting up and moving away. Weren't we going to do all those black hand motions? Wasn't he going to punch my arm or anything?

"So long, kid," he said, not looking back. "Hang in there."

Okay, Arthur, I thought, screw you. But I felt rotten. I couldn't understand what had happened, how dumb I'd been. I'd thought Arthur would always be there, every afternoon in the library, smiling when I came in.

Tonight, on my way to my typewriter in the basement, I found my mother sitting at the kitchen table. She glanced at me and then looked away. Since Dean left she looks at me as if she hardly knows me. I watched her doing nothing for a minute.

Then Papa came in and started yelling at me. He'd seen me in the park with Arthur. "What the hell were you and that nigger doing in the park?" he said. "Is he a pusher? Are you hooked on something, for Christ's sake?"

I laughed, which was stupid. He hit me hard on the side of the head. My mother didn't look up.

"That's just a sample," Papa shouted. "You stick

to your goddamn books and stay away from blacks and drugs and sluts like Annabelle. You hear?"

I came down here to the basement, but I couldn't keep from smiling at Papa's idea of Arthur. Arthur would smile too. Then I remembered.

Today I caught my mother prying quarters out of my bank with a nail file. When she saw me in the doorway, she opened her eyes wide like she does with my father.

"It's for Dean," she said. "Till he gets a job."

"No," I said, taking the bank away from her. "That's my college money."

"Come on, David, you can get more," she said, smiling like a doll. "Annabelle's brothers are after him."

I stared at her. Last week she would have yelled at me and broken the bank open.

Where can I hide the money? If you put your money in a bank, can your parents get at it? Yesterday I could have asked Arthur to keep it for me.

Tonight Papa was waiting for me when I got home. He was drinking beer and wearing his old army hat. He patted the place next to him on the couch. "Sit down, son," he said. He belched. I sat down on the edge of the couch.

"How's it all going, Dave?" he said.

"Okay. I've got homework, Papa."

"Yeah. Well. The thing is, kid, that goddamn Santini is really leaning on me," he said. "You've got to help me find Dean." He straightened his hat and put his arm around my shoulder. "We have to stick together, son."

I knew better than to laugh.

"I bet you've seen him around somewhere, haven't you?"

"No."

I knew Dean had been home because his stuff was gone.

"Well, ask around, will you?" He smiled. "Help your old man out, okay?"

I looked at his face and I felt like puking. I'd hardly ever seen him when he wasn't mad. "You want to find Dean so Santini will get off your back?"

I could see him starting to get mad, but then his shoulders slumped. "Hell, it's Dean's mess. Why should I take the rap?"

I thought about the baby then, and for the first time in my life I wished I couldn't imagine things.

I told Papa I'd look for Dean, and that scared me too. Up till then I'd been able to work things out so that I didn't have to lie like my mother.

I tried to find Dean today to make what I told Papa true. Stupid, but I did it. I wandered around the neighborhood to places where Dean used to go. Every time I saw any friends of Dean's, I was afraid I'd see him in the next second. What would I say to him? What would I tell Papa if I found him?

All the time I was looking and not looking for Dean, I was wondering how to find Arthur. Finally, I figured it out.

Everything's all right now. Or will be. The college will know where he is. I can get there on the bus.

Arthur will be glad to see me. I'm sure of that. I know he didn't really mean all that stuff he said. The first thing I'm going to do is to make him teach me what he knows. I want to look way over people's heads the way he does, even though I'm not tall. Arthur puts the whole big mess of the world where *he* wants it, where it can't hurt so much.

REFLECTIVE
A. R. Ammons

I found a
weed
that had a

mirror in it
and that
mirror

looked in at
a mirror
in

me that
had a
weed in it

SMALL SONG
A. R. Ammons

The reeds give
way to the

wind and give
the wind away

FEAR
Charles Simic

Fear passes from man to man
Unknowing,
As one leaf passes its shudder
To another.

All at once the whole tree is trembling
And there is no sign of the wind.

IF YOU CALL ME
Shirley Kaufman

If you call me on the phone
and if you tell me I'd better come
and if I put my clothes on quick
and if I run and my heart sticks
like a fish bone in my throat
and it won't go up
and it won't go down,
will you be gone?

If I run and my feet run
after me like dogs,
teeth at my heels,
my bare feet crazy
up the stairs,
will you be there?

If I run and my eyes are like gates
that open and close
and I never get
to the front of the line,
will I be on time?

BY NIGHT
Robert Francis

    After midnight I heard a scream.
    I was awake. It was no dream.
    But whether it was bird of prey
    Or prey of bird I could not say.
    I never heard that sound by day.

BABY ON THE BEACH
◆§ *Alix Kates Shulman*

I heard a baby cry. Not sadly. Not in pain. But in a panic. It was screaming, and the cry was full of panic.

I put down my work and listened. There was something wild in that cry. Something awful and wild. The cry was loud. It sounded near, almost as if the baby were there in the cabin with me. I stopped my work and walked out on the porch to listen. The sobs came louder, faster. I turned my head toward the sound. The screams hit me like blows.

From the top of the steps, at the edge of the porch, I saw him. Far below, on the beach, a small child stood alone. He seemed far away and tiny, down there on the empty beach. But his cry was loud, like a gull's cry. His sobs came louder, faster. His face was turned up to the sky. He was screaming at the sky.

He was too small to be left alone. Where were his mother, his father? Down there on the empty beach, the child was far from the road, far from the two small cabins full of summer people.

I took off, running toward the cry. I ran down the steps, my heart pounding all the way. From the bottom of the steps I couldn't see the beach or the child. But I heard him. I ran down the path from my cabin toward the beach, toward the cry.

When I got to the beach, I bent down and opened my arms. The child was still screaming. When I opened my arms, he came to me. I picked him up and held him. He was two, or maybe three. Still in Pampers. He looked at my face. Full of trust, he looked in my eyes. Then he let his head fall on my shoulder. He sobbed two or three more sobs. Then he closed his eyes, stopped crying, and seemed to drop off to sleep.

He felt sweet in my arms. His eyes were red from crying. His hair was black. His face was red and wet and soft.

"Where's your mama?" I asked.

He opened his eyes and lifted his head. "Mama, there." He pointed to the path that led up from the beach, away from the water. Toward the summer cabins behind the trees.

I looked. I saw no one. Only three gulls at the water's edge. You couldn't see the cabins from down there on the beach. You could see only the trees in front of the cabins. Again I asked, "Where's your mama?"

Again he pointed away from the water, toward the path. "Mama, there."

Still, I saw no one. I put the child down on the sand and took his hand. "Show me," I said. I wanted him to lead me to his mother. I was afraid to carry him. He felt so sweet in my arms. Like my own child. Maybe someone would think I stole him. "Show me where your mama is."

"Mama there," he said again. But he didn't go toward the path. Instead he lifted his arms. He wanted me to carry him.

"Show me," I pleaded. But he was too tired to walk. He had cried too long and too hard. He needed me to carry him.

The soft sand was hard to walk on. A wind was starting to blow. "Okay," I said. I lifted him up.

It was a long walk across that windy beach with a child in my arms. What must it feel like to him? Nothing to see but sand and water. No cabins. No road. No people. Nothing to hear but wind and gulls. Nothing to feel but sun and sand. No wonder the child felt panic. What if I hadn't come?

I started off toward the path that led past the trees. I walked slowly, feeling the sweet cheek on my shoulder, the trusting hand in my hair. "Okay," I said. I kissed his head. "We'll find your mama."

At the edge of the water, two people were walking toward us. They had come from the path, way across the beach. A young woman and a little girl.

I pointed to them.

"Is that your mama?" I asked the boy.

He opened his eyes, then shook his head.

I put him down on the sand.

"Is that your mama?" I asked again, pointing.

"No," he said.

Then he looked at me pleadingly and held up his arms. Still too tired to walk. I lifted him again and carried him toward the people.

The woman had a pretty face. She had big soft eyes, a tiny nose, and smooth red hair that fell softly to her shoulders. She had long tan legs and arms. And she was smiling.

"I'm not his mother," she said. The first thing that woman said to me was, "I'm not his mother." Smiling, she ran her hand across her long red hair.

"Do you like that baby?" asked the little girl. "His name is Tony."

The woman looked down at the girl and smiled. "Oh, are you giving Tony away?"

Tony's arms held fast to my neck; his head still rested on my shoulder. I held on to him. "Where is his mother, then?" I asked. "He's pretty upset."

"Oh, it's not as bad as it looks," said the woman. "He's okay. His mother is my friend. They just came out to the beach for the day. It's okay."

It didn't look okay to me. The woman didn't hold out her arms to Tony. She didn't even look at him. She looked only at me.

"It was my idea," she said. "I told his mother to leave him there. He was acting awful. He didn't want to walk. He wanted to be carried. He was crying and screaming. He was so bad. He just wouldn't stop. So I said, Let's just keep walking and see how long he carries on like this. He can't keep it up all day. So we walked on home."

I stared at her. Crying was *bad?* "But he didn't know where you were," I said. "He couldn't see you."

"He couldn't see us, but we could see him from the cabin."

I looked at her, smoothing her hair with her hand, smiling. I shook my head. Who could leave a baby alone to panic on a strange beach? My heart was pounding again. I was getting more and more upset. But I didn't say any more. What could I say? Words would add nothing. The woman was upset. What did she think? She never stopped smiling. She never looked at the child. She looked only at me.

I handed Tony to the woman. She took him without a word. He went smoothly into her arms. She didn't try to put him down. Full of trust, he didn't even look back.

"Take care of him," I said.

"Tony, say bye-bye," said the little girl. "Blow a kiss, Tony," she said. But Tony's head was on the woman's shoulder, and he didn't look back.

The wind had started up again. From my porch I looked down on the empty beach. Only the gulls over the water were crying now.

STILLS
A. R. Ammons

I have nowhere
to go and

nowhere to go

when I get
back from there

SEPARATION
W. S. Merwin

Your absence has gone through me
Like thread through a needle.
Everything I do is stitched with its color.

WHEN MY FATHER DIED
Sharon Olds

When my father died, I was there in the room.
His wife was at the sink washing her hands,
the nurse was down the hall. I was alone
with my father. He was lying on his back, his spine
   was
bending and bending so he seemed to be lifting his
head to speak to me. His skin
white-gold, his eyes half closed, his
mouth open, he looked like a large
puzzled mouse, one pulled from the pool and
laid on the tile to curl in the sun with its
paws up. I leaned to him,
he took a small breath, for a moment it
sat on his tongue in a small puff,
then the breath came out by itself,
then he lay there, lifted up,
still, silent. I stole a minute for myself,
I stroked his skin, I had never been
alone with him. I bent above him,
big man, not a talker,
the one I had loved best. I gave myself
half a minute alone with his flesh

free of spirit—as if I were feeding on a
god. I gazed at his face and body, then
called out quietly, and the others turned and
came toward the bed like the petals of a flower
closing, turning back into a bud, a
stem, a sprout, a place in the dirt, one
spot on the huge, rough seed of the earth.

WHILE I SLEPT
Robert Francis

While I slept, while I slept and the night grew colder
She would come to my room, stepping softly
And draw a blanket about my shoulder
While I slept.

While I slept, while I slept in the dark still heat,
She would come to my bedside, stepping coolly,
And smooth the twisted, troubled sheet
While I slept.

Now she sleeps, sleeps under quiet rain
While nights grow warm or nights grow colder.
And I wake, and sleep, and wake again
While she sleeps.

NEXT DOOR
Vesle Fenstermaker

On the afternoon of your death
a light rain is falling.

Later I will grieve.
Now I hurry from my back door to yours,
slipping on wet moss.

Inside your kitchen
every shining surface
reflects you
with a cloth in your hand,
cleaning, cleaning.

Way in the back of a lower cupboard,
lined with glossy paper,
I find the terrible roasting pan.

Yes. Marred and blackened here and there,
and I feel again your hand on my arm
as you ask me,
pretending to laugh at yourself,

to remove it
on this day,
the minute I hear.

Well, it's gone now.
Safe, like you, from sorting relatives.

Somehow, I'm smiling.
Are you?

CAROLINE
Linda Pastan

She wore
her coming death
as gracefully
as if it were a coat
she'd learn to sew.
When it grew cold enough
she'd simply button it
and go.

ADAM'S COMPLAINT
Denise Levertov

Some people,
no matter what you give them,
still want the moon.

The bread,
the salt,
white meat and dark,
still hungry.

The marriage bed
and the cradle,
still empty arms.

You give them land,
their own earth under their feet,
still they take to the roads.

And water: dig them the deepest well,
still it's not deep enough
to drink the moon from.

BOARDING HOUSE
Ted Kooser

The blind man draws his curtains for the night
and goes to bed, leaving a burning light

above the bathroom mirror. Through the wall,
he hears the deaf man walking down the hall

in his squeaky shoes to see if there's a light
under the blind man's door, and all is right.

A VERY SPECIAL CHRISTMAS
Nikki Giovanni

When I was a little girl we lived in an apartment in a small Ohio town. My parents were teaching school then, and Daddy had a second job because he had a growing family and all, and we were trying to save enough money to buy a house. All of us were looking forward to a house because I had been promised a back-yard for kickball, Mommy would have a real living room, Gary, my big sister, could have a dog, and Daddy could have peace and quiet.

Gary was always running around with her friends and all—but I was Mommy's child, which being a girl, worked out, because I became a real good cook. Gary and her friends were always doing something and going someplace with each other on their bikes. I didn't really want to go anyway, so it was no big thing to me. Plus I didn't have a bike and I was scared to ask, because I always hung around the house and I always heard them talking about bills, saving money, and people who were going to take things back.

It didn't seem fair to be asking for something when you already knew they didn't have any money for the things we already had. When all the kids at school had been talking about having TVs and we didn't have one, Gus, that's my daddy, found out that we all felt bad, so he went and got one. I figured I shouldn't ask for anything else, even though there were other things I thought it would be nifty to have.

That Christmas my sister got a new bike because she had outgrown her old one. I had asked Santa for skates. It was sunny that day, and when I went back upstairs Mommy and Daddy could tell something was wrong. When Daddy asked how I liked my skates, I told him fine and how fast I could go. Daddy saw that I was about to cry. He asked if Santa had maybe made a mistake by bringing me skates and bringing Gary a bike.

I didn't think it was my place to criticize Santa for bringing me what I had asked for, so I just told Daddy I was tired and wanted to play inside with my other toys.

I went to my bedroom and started working on one of my puzzles, when I heard Daddy say to my mother, "I'm not going to take this. We'll just get this child a bike." And Mommy said, "But, Gus, where can you get one today?" And Daddy said, "Somebody will sell me a bike today."

Then he came in and said, "Nikki, put on your coat. We're going to get you a bike." I didn't see that he could really get me one, but he didn't ask my opinion.

Daddy and Mommy and I got in the car and went out to find one. None of the stores looked open, but when Daddy pulled up to the store with rows and rows of beautiful bikes, a man was standing in the door.

The man said, "I wouldn't do this for anybody but you." And Daddy smiled and told me to pick out a bike. I knew right away which one I wanted, but I thought it was only proper to give all the other bikes a fair chance. I walked up and down for what seemed like forever and then came back to the speedy-looking blue one. It was almost as big as Gary's, and I just knew I could keep up with her and her friends. Daddy shook hands with the salesman, and Mommy asked if I was happy. I was the happiest child in the whole world, and nobody could tell me different.

When we got home, Gary and all her friends were waiting for us, to see if I really did get two big presents for Christmas. Daddy took the bike off the roof of the car and set it down. It was the most beautiful bike in the world. Daddy looked at it and looked at me for what seemed like a long time. I was afraid I had done something wrong and that now I wouldn't be allowed to keep it.

"Nikki?" he asked. "Yes, Gus?" "Do you know how to ride a bike?" "Yes, Gus." "Okay. Let me see you." And he stood there while I whizzed down the street and back. He smiled (which he rarely does) and told Mommy, "Well, I'll be damned." Then they went back upstairs. All the kids came around to look at my second big Christmas present, and I felt very special and like a for-real big girl. And Gary even said I could go riding with her.

The World in Your Hands

PAINTING THE GATE
May Swenson

I painted the mailbox. That was fun.
I painted it postal blue.

Then I painted the gate.

I painted a spider that got on the gate.
I painted his mate.

I painted the ivy around the gate.
Some stones I painted blue,
and part of the cat as he rubbed by.

I painted my hair. I painted my shoe.

I painted the slats, both front and back,
all their beveled edges too.
I painted the numbers on the gate.
I shouldn't have, but it was too late.
I painted the posts, each side and top.
I painted the hinges, the handle, the lock,
several ants, and a moth asleep in a crack.

At last I was through.

I'd painted the gate
shut, me out, with both hands dark blue,
as well as my nose which,
early on, because of a sudden itch,
got painted. But wait!
I had painted the gate.

AT THE PLAYGROUND
William Stafford

Away down deep and away up high,
a swing drops you into the sky.

Back, it draws you away down deep,
forth, it flings you in a sweep

all the way to the stars and back
—Goodbye, Jill; Goodbye, Jack:

shuddering climb, wild and steep,
away up high, away down deep.

FREEDOM MARCH
~§ *Adapted by Dick Gregory from his book* Nigger

"What are you going to do if they spit in your face, if they hit you, if they knock you down?" an old man asked me. "Are you going to hit back?"

"I'm going to try not to."

The old man shook his head. "We can't use you."

"You can't use me? Why the hell not?"

"Mister Gregory, you got to *know* you're not going to fight back."

I couldn't believe I was standing there on a Greenwood street and listening to an old Mississippi Negro, a man I had come down to do a favor for, tell me he couldn't use me. I told him I'd have to think about it. He nodded his nappy old head and said he'd be back, and shuffled away.

It was the spring of 1962. The nonviolent civil rights movement inspired by Dr. Martin Luther King, Jr., was getting under way. I had come down from New York City to Greenwood, Mississippi, to take part in the demonstrations, and I was being told that I had a few things to learn about nonviolent action.

There were no demonstrations that first day, but I spoke to a crowded church rally that night. Although there were fifteen Negro churches in Greenwood, only two of them had opened their doors to the demonstrators. I stood up there and told that crowd how the Negro preachers had brought us all the way to the battle lines and then had abandoned us. They were scared of losing their jobs, of having their churches bombed, of coming up empty in the collection plates. Many of our churches were failing us in this battle for civil rights. I told them that it was the preachers' fault that whenever we made a gain we said, "Thank the United States Supreme Court," instead of saying, "Thank God."

I looked at those people in that church, those beautiful people who were taking chances with their lives, with what little they had in the world. There wasn't a single Negro doctor in Greenwood. When Negroes demonstrate, they run the chance that no white doctor will treat them. A Negro couldn't even afford to get sick. And now they were going out, maybe to die, without any of their local Negro leaders. The preachers were scared, the Negro schoolteachers and principals were too afraid for their jobs to go out on the streets.

That night, standing in front of those people, I told them I'd be proud to lead them the following day. I really hadn't planned to lead the marching, but looking at those beautiful faces ready to die for freedom, I knew I couldn't do less.

The next morning, while we were getting ready to

march on the courthouse, that old man who had come up to me the day before walked over to me.

"We're ready to go, Mr. Gregory. What do you think?"

By that time I was beginning to understand what he had meant. "Okay, I'll do it."

So we marched. Old people, kids, voter registration workers, women. We started off, and with every step I was scared, waiting for that bullet to come from a rooftop, waiting for that car to come by and shoot me from the ground.

The police stopped us after one block and told us we couldn't parade through the city. Dozens of policemen with clubs and guns began pushing the marchers around. The next thing I knew, someone had twisted my arm behind my back and was pushing me across the street. It was a Greenwood policeman.

"Move on, nigger."

"Thanks a million."

"Thanks for what?"

"Up North, police don't escort me across the street against a red light."

"I said move on, nigger."

"I don't know my way. I'm new in this town."

The cop yanked on my arm and turned his head. "Send someone over here to show this nigger where to go," he hollered. The press and the cameramen moved in and out of the crowds of white men and women and children standing on the street corners. I pulled one of

The World in Your Hands 91

my arms free and pointed into the crowd. "Ask that white woman over there to come here and show me where to go."

The cop's face got red, and there was spittle at the corner of his mouth. All he could say was: "Nigger, dirty nigger . . . you damned black monkey."

"Who you calling a monkey? Monkey's got thin lips, monkey's got blue eyes and straight hair."

He dropped my other arm then and backed away, his hand on his gun. I thought he was going to explode. But nothing happened. I was sopping wet and too excited to be scared. He made a motion, and two other cops grabbed me and threw me into the back of a police car. One of them asked the driver, "You want any help with this nigger?"

"Why do you always think a Negro's going to hurt somebody? Close the door and let this fool take me to jail."

The cop who was driving turned around and started slapping at my head. I held my hands over my face. "Get your hands down, nigger," he yelled, and kept swinging at my head. He didn't do much damage. Then he started the car and drove about three blocks, away from everything. He pulled the car over to the curb, and when he turned around again he was crying.

"My God, what are you trying to do to me?" he said. He sat in the car and he looked at me and told me that when he was at home at night his kids looked at him funny, that they made him feel bad. I sat there and I couldn't believe that I was hearing these words from a white cop who had been hitting me and niggering me a minute before. He said, "As right as you are—you're down here helping these people—I got to stop you and I can't do it. Sometimes I think you are a better man than I am."

He didn't take me to jail. He drove me back to our headquarters. I got out of the car and handed him two dollars.

"What's this for?"

"I always tip chauffeurs. Hell, if you don't take me to jail, you're my chauffeur."

From there I rushed back to the demonstration, but the parade was over. So we did exactly what the cops had been screaming at us to do. We broke up in twos and threes and went off quietly in different directions.

POLITICIAN
❧ *John Keeble*

The politician had come to the Holiday Inn. The motel was next to the Interstate just outside a town in Wyoming. It was summertime and hot, rattlesnake weather in the wild, empty country.

Everything was big—the sky, the rocks, the cliffs, and the dark canyons. Here and there in the distance were soft, gray clouds shaped like mushrooms. They came from the mines. Some of the clouds were not far from town, while others were two or three hundred miles away. A person could see forever here.

In front of the Holiday Inn was an awning, held up by a concrete wall. It made a shady place to park a car. There was a blue sign that said: LOADING ZONE. 5 MINUTE PARKING. The politician's long, white limousine stood in the middle of the space, so nobody else could use it even for turning around. The limousine was shiny like whole milk. It had dark windows and a fancy antenna. A sign in one window said: OFFICIAL.

The motel parking lot was full of cars. A van from the TV station was pulled up near the awning. Through the glass doors of the entryway to the motel, waitresses could be seen going back and forth, again and again.

They carried trays of food from the kitchen to the big meeting room. That's where the politician was, inside that room behind a pair of double doors.

The room was crammed with people, more people by far than there were places to sit. This was because the politician was going to make an important announcement that had to do with the railroad and the mines. Everybody around here depended on the mines. If your money didn't come from work in the mines, then it came from selling something to people whose money did, or maybe from a relief fund. There was black lung disease among the people, and a lot of bad backs and missing hands. There were one-legged men from the old days.

The mines were big, but the railroad was bigger yet. One way or another, the railroad owned the mines. The politician got his start working in the offices of the railroad. The railroad owned huge chunks of land from when it first laid down tracks over a hundred years ago. It opened its own coal mine back then. The coal was burned in the steam engines. Later, other things were mined and other companies came in, but you couldn't move anything in or out of any of the mines except by railroad car. The railroad controlled the bank, too, and held the deeds to most of the land the town was built upon. This is the truth. These were not good times. Workers were being laid off, and people were anxious to learn if the politician would have better news for them or more of the bad.

People were still arriving at the motel, flocks of

them. Now they had to park out on the street, walk across the lot, come by the limousine, go through the glass entryway, and then try to get into the meeting room. A crowd built up outside the double doors of the meeting room and began to fill the motel lobby, which made it hard for the waitresses to do their work.

A chauffeur watched over the limousine. He stood outside, leaning against a rear fender. His arms were crossed. Maybe he was also looking through the glass doors into the lobby. It was hard to be sure, because of his dark sunglasses. His face was like rock.

The people who passed him might nod. Everyone took a look at the limousine, of course. Some seemed as though they were about to say something to the chauffeur, but then they wouldn't. The chauffeur didn't move a muscle. Normally, folks here are friendly. Strangers don't scare them at all, but there was something about the limousine and chauffeur that kept them from being themselves.

The chauffeur wore a black suit, black tie, and black boots. He had a silver belt buckle with a red stone in the center. He wore a black hat and black leather gloves. It was hot to be wearing such clothes. He had a moustache. He was tall and powerful looking. He didn't move. He was as still as a lizard.

The crowd grew larger out here. Some came outside from the motel. They had given up trying to get in the room to hear what the politician had to say. A few latecomers didn't even try to go inside. The people squeezed between the limousine and the motel entryway, but no one got too close to the limousine. It was quiet, so quiet that engines could be heard from the mines in the distance. The people were waiting, waiting for something to happen, waiting for the news. It seemed that they were breathing together, as if in church. Some began fanning themselves with newspapers.

Finally, the chauffeur moved. First he stretched out his left arm and looked at his watch, then he walked around the front of the car. His boots made a crunching sound in the sand on the concrete. He stopped and took off one glove. His hand was as pale as a fish. All heads turned in his direction. He pulled a white handkerchief from his pocket and leaned over the hood like he was going to kiss it. You could see his black reflection in the shiny, milk-colored paint. He reached out with the handkerchief and carefully rubbed at a spot. He looked like a surgeon, taking out that spot no one but him could see.

He straightened up, returned the handkerchief to his pocket, and put his glove back on. He walked around to the driver's side and opened the door. He leaned inside and pushed a button. At the back of the car, the trunk clicked open. The chauffeur walked to the trunk and took out a small, chrome-plated vacuum cleaner with a black dust bag. It must have been battery powered.

He moved to the rear door on the far side of the car, opened it, bent in, and started vacuuming. Nobody could see him over on that side of the car near the concrete wall, and yet everybody watched. The vacuum cleaner whirred softly. In a few minutes, the chauffeur came out. He walked around to this side, opened the rear door, and leaned inside. Now the people could see his shoulders moving and his powerful legs pumping slowly as he worked. He had brand-new heels on his boots. Some could see inside the car: the black carpet, black leather seats, TV screen, a sink, a row of whiskey bottles on a shelf, and the chrome vacuum cleaner gliding back and forth.

At about this time, a voice called out, "Coming through!" Everyone looked around. Sue Wyse appeared. She moved into the space between the people and the car, then jumped back a little and said, "Whoa!" She looked around, smiling broadly. A few people smiled back at her.

Sue worked for the motel as a gardener. She carried a shovel and a bucket of cow manure. In all these years, folks still hadn't learned what to make of Sue. She didn't care. She was a bit simple. Folks were fond of her and watched out for her because it was easy to take advantage of her. She lived on the edge of everything, but she always did what people said. If two people told her to do opposite things, she would try to please them both.

Someone said, "Hey, Sue."

Sue set down her bucket and raised her hand. "Hi there," she said in her sweet voice.

She wore overalls and rubber boots. She was a large woman with frizzy black hair and happy, foolish eyes. She was pretty in a strange way. Now she had an earth-colored stain on one cheek. She also wore a T-shirt, and just above the bib of her overalls was a big red word—ALMOST. Under the bib were the rest of the words, which nobody could see, and it made a person wonder—ALMOST what? She moved close to the chauffeur and looked inside the car. She spoke to the chauffeur. It sounded as if she were asking him a question. Maybe she wanted to go for a ride in the limousine, or maybe she wanted to try out the vacuum cleaner.

The chauffeur backed out of the car and stood up straight. He turned his head toward Sue and held it there.

"What does the senator believe? That's what I asked," Sue said.

The chauffeur didn't speak.

"What does he believe is best for us?" Sue said.

Still the chauffeur didn't speak.

Sue raised one hand, held it out, and it sounded as if she was about to cry. "What should we do?"

Half of the chauffeur's mouth snaked out sideways. It was a smile. The two of them were looking at each other. Sue hung on to her shovel and the chauffeur held his vacuum cleaner. The chauffeur had one of those faces that could look like anything you wanted. For a brief moment, he looked as foolish as Sue, like she'd hooked him and pulled him into her world, but then the smile disappeared from his face. He placed one finger between the M and O in ALMOST and pushed. She had to step back. The chauffeur moved around her, shut the door, and

The World in Your Hands

walked to the back of the limousine. He put the vacuum cleaner away and touched a button on the lid of the trunk. The lid automatically sucked shut and locked itself.

Sue continued on her way, working through the crowd. She looked hurt. When she went out from the shade of the awning, her shovel flashed in the sun. Her body tipped to one side because of the weight of the loaded bucket. The chauffeur came back to his place at the fender. He crossed his arms. The red stone on his belt buckle shone. He turned to watch as Sue moved along the side of the motel toward a line of young trees. He had hate in his face.

"ALMOST as dumb as we are," a man in the crowd said bitterly.

"But only ALMOST," a woman said.

Others began to talk in low voices.

The chauffeur stretched out his arm and looked at his watch. He walked around the car again and opened the front door, slid in, and started the engine. The limousine purred. The chauffeur got out and shut the door. He came back and stood there facing the glass entryway. He looked like death. Inside, the waitresses were fighting their way through the crowd. They were trying to carry trays full of dirty dishes back to the kitchen. The crowd churned around, this way and that. People were pressed against the walls. Suddenly the double doors burst open.

A knot of tall men, the local party leaders, came first. People poured after them. In the middle of the knot of men was the politician, but all anyone could see of him was the top of his bald head. The knot moved toward the limousine. The crowd swung wildly back and forth. A woman fell down, and other people were forced out into the parking lot. The reporter from the local TV station ran after the knot of men. He held up a microphone and shouted, "Senator! Senator! What about the mines?"

With a brutal movement, the chauffeur jerked open the rear door of the limousine. The politician's head flashed like a dime, then passed into the darkness. The door closed. The chauffeur walked around and got in behind the wheel. The crowd pressed close to the car as it pulled forward. Some even chased it across the parking lot. The car pulled into the street, then went up to the Interstate. In a moment, the car turned into a tiny white dot. In another moment, it had disappeared into the big, empty country. The people gathered in small groups to talk. Sue could be heard grunting as she dug in the black manure around the roots of the trees.

LIGHTS
Stuart Dybek

In summer, waiting for night, we'd pose against the afterglow on corners, watching traffic cruise through the neighborhood. Sometimes a car would go by without its headlights on, and we'd all yell, "Lights!"

"Lights!" we'd keep yelling until the beams flashed on. It was usually immediate—the driver would honk back thanks, or flinch embarrassed behind the steering wheel, or speed past, and we'd see his red taillights blink on.

But there were times—who knows why?—when drunk or high, stubborn, or simply lost in that glide to somewhere else, the driver just kept driving in the dark, and all down the block we'd hear yelling from doorways and storefronts, front steps and other corners, voices winking on like fireflies: "Lights! Your *lights!* Hey, lights!"

BRANDY'S STORY
Ted Solotaroff

When I saw Wayne, Shadow, and Richard hanging out in the subway, I knew something was up. That's their street names I'm telling you. Wayne is really James. I don't know who Shadow is really. Richard, though, is just Richard.

Wayne is built, and he's got little mean eyes, like rat's eyes, that stare at you. I always thought Wayne was scary, but Rhonda, who used to be his girlfriend, said he was all right if you didn't cross him. That's what she said before all that I'm telling you happened.

Shadow looks like he's about twelve, but he's really seventeen, like Wayne. Lots of kids on the block don't look their real age. Some look younger like Shadow, though some look years older, like me. Shadow looks dopey too, like he's out of it. But he's got fast feet. Even when he's sitting down, you think of him running and dodging. He's called Shadow because he's always hanging out with Wayne, not because of the quick way he moves.

Shadow and Wayne have been ripping people off for a couple of years. Shadow stops them. They figure they got nothing to fear from this little kid, then along comes Wayne out of nowhere and mugs them. That's how they do it.

Richard I can't figure out. He's different. He's smart, like me. He's still in high school and probably could graduate and study computers or something. And his folks still live together. They got a nice place around the corner on Riverside Drive. Richard's got slanty brown eyes and a sweet smile and a nice long bod, all legs, and skin like mocha ice cream. Sometimes when I watch Richard, something in me says, Oh my! But it's like he's not into girls, or even knows he's got all that going for him. He frowns and tries to look bad. When he's with the crowd, his eyes are always going this way and that, like he's expecting someone to start something that he don't know if he can deal with.

It was late, maybe one-thirty. I know that because we were sitting on the cars, Rhonda and me, and she looked at her watch and said it was past one o'clock, so Dirk wasn't going to show. She said he had probably run into something downtown. Dirk is 22 and has his own place. Sometimes Rhonda and me and a couple of the other kids go up there and smoke and maybe do some coke if Dirk feels like fooling around. Dirk's nice. We know we can trust him, like he's not going to give us angel dust or any shit like that. He comes on to Rhonda sometimes when his own girl, Bucky, is working downtown, but he doesn't with me. He says I'm too young even to be called Brandy. He says it gives guys ideas. Dirk is sort of like everybody's big brother.

I tell Rhonda I better go home in case my grandmoms is waiting up for me. Gram lives over in the Project near my school. I been staying with her this summer because Moms left the block and started living way uptown with her new husband, Miles. There's only room there for my little brother—actually my half-brother—Jesse. My real brother, Martin, has a couple of girls he lives with over in Harlem. I hear about him from Dirk, who sees him around in the clubs sometimes. He says Martin is doing just fine. Moms can't take what's happened to him though, after he went to Bronx Community College and all to be a lawyer. But that's another story.

Rhonda walks me to our subway. That's when I see Wayne and Shadow and Richard up by the booth, hanging loose with their supercool look. They're waiting to jump the turnstile, but you wouldn't know it.

I pay my fare and go on down to the tracks, and a few minutes later Wayne and Shadow and Richard are coming down the stairs, following this little fat guy. When they come past me, Wayne looks weird. He makes his eyes real mean and says, "You don't know anyone here, got it?" Then I notice all three of them look really weird. I figure maybe they just finished doing some crack. Richard says, "Get out of here, Brandy. Go back to the block." But Shadow tells him, "She's already seen, so it don't make no difference." Then he starts this dopey laughing for no reason, and I know it's crack for sure. Nothing else works that fast.

Then Wayne says to get the hell out, but I tell him I'm staying right where I am. "I know what you're here for," I say. "You want to rip someone off. So just keep away from me." But I move off about ten feet anyway and turn my back on them. I figure that what I don't see is no business of mine. I wanted to say something to Richard, but it wouldn't do any good coming from me. Anyway, when I look around he is walking back up the stairs. Then I see Shadow hand something to Wayne, and I see then it's a gun. Wayne puts it in the pocket of his jeans and the handle bulges out. You could tell by the way he walked he felt heavy packing heat.

I decide that whatever is going to happen with that gun, I don't want to be part of it. I start walking back toward the stairs. If Richard is still hanging around up there, I might tell him about the gun in case he doesn't know.

Just then the train comes. That's how they do it. They wait for the train, and just before it comes, they rip the chump off fast and jump on the train and are gone. By the time the guy can tell anyone, Wayne and Shadow have gotten off and split. Sometimes they wait a couple of stops. It depends.

Well, I'm starting up the stairs when I hear this sound like a big firecracker. When I look around, Shadow is running toward me. Right behind him is Wayne, holding the gun. And behind them the little fat man is all bent over, holding his stomach. Then he falls down.

Wayne and Shadow tear through the gate. The lady in the change booth says what happened and I tell her there's this guy downstairs who needs help. She gets on the special phone she's got and tells me to wait because the police are coming. So I split too.

Back on the block, Rhonda is still sitting out on the cars. I tell her what happened, and we decide to call my Moms even if it means waking her up. I tell Moms how Wayne and Shadow shot someone, and she says stay right there and don't tell anyone anything. Then she asks me was I scared, and I say I'm all right. Actually, I don't feel that great, especially if I think about the little fat guy. I keep seeing him, like in slow motion, the way he folded up and fell over. He must have been dead to fall like that. If he is dead, that would be the ninth dead person I've seen, not counting my aunt Bess and a kid from my class. They were both in coffins.

Moms comes and takes me right up to her place. She says I've got myself in a real mess now, and everything's going to change. One, I'll be living uptown with her for the rest of the summer. Two, I can't hang out on the block anymore. Three, I have a curfew of nine o'-clock.

But it didn't do any good keeping me away from the block. About a week ago, this detective called Jerry came to Moms' house and asked a lot of questions. First Moms did most of the talking, trying to find out what he knew. Then he told Moms to get me out of the room for a while. When they called me back, Moms said, "You better tell him everything you saw. They already know all about it."

Jerry was real cool to talk to. He looks a lot like Richard Pryor, and you'd never think he was a cop. He knew everything about the neighborhood, like even about Dirk and the parties at his place. He told me to keep away from Dirk; that in another year or so he would try to put me out on the street.

What I was doing talking to him was kind of mixed up in my mind. I mean it was scary ratting on Wayne and Shadow—especially Wayne—and I felt bad for Richard, who, it turns out, was only their lookout. But it felt good not to have it for a secret anymore. Also Jerry told me the little fat guy wasn't going to die, so even if they did time, it wouldn't be for life.

I asked if they would put Wayne in prison right away. Jerry said not for a while, but Wayne wouldn't know I had talked to him. Like Moms, he said I shouldn't tell anyone anything. When I said what about Rhonda, he said he'd already talked to her, and she was cool.

So I wasn't that scared anymore. It was like Jerry would take care of me now. There's Moms too, of course, but it's better when there is a man. Jerry gives me a feeling I never had before. Moms' husbands are mostly like Miles, nice for a while, but you can tell from the start they got more on their mind than you. Miles said I should get myself a job for the summer to take my mind off what had happened. I told him I was too young to get working papers. He said I sure didn't look twelve, which is true. Except that doesn't help with getting working papers.

Then yesterday Wayne called me. Lucky Moms was home so I handed her the phone. She said right off, "Wayne why did you want to shoot that man in front of Brandy?" Then she said, "Whether she was out too late by herself has nothing to do with it." Wayne said something else and Moms said, "Fooling around? You call shooting a man in the stomach just fooling around?" They talked some more and Moms said, "Brandy isn't going to the neighborhood anymore and you'd better not put you feet in this one if you know what's good for you. If you try to call her again, I'm going to the police about you."

But I don't know. Before I went to sleep last night I saw those mean eyes and that crazy look Wayne has when he's hurting someone. Crack can make him do anything.

It's nice around Seaman Avenue with the park and the river and the clean streets. But nothing much is going on here at night. Moms says that in another year I'll be ready to go to George Washington High School. She says it's almost like a honky school and will give me much more chance to make something of myself. But I sure wish they'd have that trial and send Wayne to prison so I can hang out with Rhonda on the block again.

AFTER A WINTER'S SILENCE
May Sarton

Along the terrace wall
Snowdrops have pushed through
Hard ice, making a pool.
Delicate stems now show
White bells as though
The force, the thrust to flower
Were nothing at all.
Who gives them the power?

After a winter's silence
I feel the shock of spring.
My breath warms like the sun,
Melts ice, bursts into song.
So when that inner one
Gives life back the power
To rise up and push through,
There's nothing to it.
We simply have to do it,
As snowdrops know
When snowdrops flower.

COPYRIGHT ACKNOWLEDGMENTS

"To Recite Every Day" and "Loyalty." From *An Oregon Message* by William Stafford. Copyright © 1987 by William Stafford. Reprinted by permission of Harper & Row, Publishers, Inc.

"Elegy." Adapted from *The Men in My Life* by James D. Houston. Copyright © 1987 by James D. Houston. Reprinted by permission of the author.

"Invitation." Copyright © 1990 by Sally Ann Drucker.

"What I Want," "The Arch," and "If You Call Me." Copyright © 1990 by Shirley Kaufman.

"Lovers in Middle Age." Copyright © 1990 by Donald Hall.

"In January, 1962." From *One World at a Time* by Ted Kooser. Copyright © 1985 by Ted Kooser. Reprinted by permission of the University of Pittsburgh Press.

"The Widow Lester" and "Boarding House." From *Sure Signs* by Ted Kooser. Copyright © 1980 by Ted Kooser. Reprinted by permission of the University of Pittsburgh Press.

"He Said:" From *Goodnight Willie Lee, I'll See You in the Morning* by Alice Walker. Copyright © 1979 by Alice Walker. Reprinted by permission of Doubleday, a division of Bantam, Doubleday, Dell Publishing Group, Inc., and by permission of David Higham Associates Ltd. Published in England by The Women's Press.

"And That Was It." Copyright © 1990 by Sharon Thompson.

"Housecleaning" and "Alone." From *The Women and the Men* by Nikki Giovanni. Copyright © 1975 by Nikki Giovanni. Reprinted by permission of the author.

"Market Adviser" and "Stills." Copyright © 1990 by A. R. Ammons.

"Apple Core." Copyright © 1990 by Clarence Major.

"First Light." Adapted from *First Light* by Charles Baxter. Copyright © 1987 by Charles Baxter. Reprinted by permission of Viking Penguin, a division of Penguin Books USA, Inc., and by permission of the Liz Darhansoff Agency.

"Happiness." Copyright © 1990 by Stephen Dunn.

"Goodbye, Shep." Copyright © 1969 by Vesle Fenstermaker. Used by permission of the author.

"In Memory of Our Cat, Ralph." From *We Are Still Married* by Garrison Keillor. Copyright © 1988 by Garrison Keillor. Reprinted by permission of Viking Penguin USA and by permission of the author.

"After Conversation." From *One-Eyed Cat* by Paula Fox. Copyright © 1984 by Paula Fox. Reprinted by permission of Bradbury Press, an Affiliate of Macmillan, Inc.

"Stranger." Copyright © 1990 by Donald Hall. Used by permission of the author.

"To Stella." Copyright © 1990 by John Hollander.

"The Night Your Dress Lifted" and "Lights." Copyright © 1990 by Stuart Dybek.

"Cover Me Over." From *Collected Poems 1930–1986* by Richard Eberhardt. Copyright © 1960, 1976, 1988 by Richard Eberhardt. Reprinted by permission of Oxford University Press, Inc.

"Where Arthur Is." Copyright © 1976 by Vesle Fenstermaker. Used by permission of the author.

"Reflective" and "Small Song." Reprinted from *The Selected Poems, 1951–1977*, by A. R. Ammons, by permission of W. W. Norton & Company, Inc. Copyright © 1977, 1975, 1974, 1972, 1971, 1970, 1966, 1965, 1964, 1955 by A. R. Ammons.

"Fear." From *Selected Poems* by Charles Simic. Copyright © 1985 by Charles Simic. Reprinted by permission of George Braziller, Publishers, Inc., and by Martin Secker & Warburg Limited.

"By Night" and "While I Slept." From *Robert Francis: Collected Poems, 1936–1976* by Robert Francis. Copyright © 1936, 1964 by Robert Francis. Reprinted by permission of the University of Massachusetts Press.

"Baby on the Beach." Copyright © 1990 by Alix Kates Shulman.

"Separation." From *Poetry* by W. S. Merwin. Copyright © 1962, 1963 by W. S. Merwin. Reprinted by permission of Atheneum Publishers, an imprint of Macmillan Publishing Company, and of Georges Borchardt, Inc., and the author.

"When My Father Died." Copyright © 1990 by Sharon Olds.

"Next Door." Copyright © 1987 by Vesle Fenstermaker. Used by permission of the author.

"Caroline." Reprinted from *The Five Stages of Grief: Poems* by Linda Pastan, by permission of the author and W. W. Norton & Company, Inc. Copyright © 1978 by Linda Pastan.

"Adam's Complaint." From *Poems, 1968–1972* by Denise Levertov. Copyright © 1970 by Denise Levertov Goodman. Reprinted by permission of New Directions Publishing Corporation.

"A Very Special Christmas." Copyright © 1990 by Nikki Giovanni. Reprinted by permission of the author.

"Painting the Gate." Copyright © 1976 by May Swenson. Reprinted by permission of the author.

"At the Playground." From *Stories That Could Be True* by William Stafford. Copyright © 1977 by William Stafford. Reprinted by permission of Harper & Row, Publishers, Inc.

"Freedom March." Adapted from *Nigger: An Autobiography* by Dick Gregory with Robert Lipsyte. Copyright © 1964 by Dick Gregory. Reprinted by permission of the author.

"Politician." Copyright © 1990 by John Keeble.

"Lights." Copyright © 1990 by Stuart Dybek.

"Brandy's Story." Copyright © 1990 by Ted Solotaroff.

"After a Winter's Silence." From *Letters from Maine: New Poems* by May Sarton. Copyright © 1984 by May Sarton. Reprinted by permission of W. W. Norton & Company, Inc., and by Russell & Volkening, Inc., as agent for the author.